The Sea, The Sea

Rosemarie Jarski

NEW HOLLAND

There's magic in water that draws all men away from
the land, that leads them over the hills, down creeks
and streams and rivers to the sea.
Herman Melville

The sea has always had an irresistible allure for mankind. Not
surprising, for we are all children of the ocean. Salt water flows
through our veins, we weep salty tears, our souls are inextricably
bound with the briny. People who live by the sea attest to the powerful
bond they develop with their aquatic surroundings. They fall naturally
into the rhythms of the ocean. Their hearts beat in synchrony with the
tides. People who live by the sea know the meaning of eternity.

For those of us not lucky enough to have a home by the ocean, an
ideal holiday is usually one spent beside the sea. We can all name a
favourite image or memory of the sea in our lives. It may be collecting
shells by the seashore, a solitary walk along a windswept coastline, or
strolling with a lover on a deserted bay. *The Sea, The Sea* invites you to
slip the moorings of the daily grind, and go down to the sea again, to
relive those cherished memories and reawaken many more.

From a rhapsody in blue to a symphony in silver, the sea has voices to satisfy all our moods. It can be a playground for fun, a temple for quiet reflection, a hunting-ground for romance, a stadium for sports or a launch pad for adventure (who has not fantasized about running away to sea?). Recreation, inspiration, love, solace, mystery and escape, what theme park offers as many thrills as the sea? As we grow older, the sea also appeals to our sense of nostalgia, evoking memories of bucket-and-spade-holidays with sand in the sandwiches, wasps in the tea and—if you're holidaying in Britain, rain just about every place else.

Our vision of the sea has inevitably been coloured by what has been written about it. From the cradle, our imaginations are fired by fairy tales like *The Little Mermaid* and swashbuckling tales of derring-do on the high seas. Romantic poets like Byron, Shelley and Swinburne shape our sense of the sea as a source of the Sublime – an awesome power revealing our own insignificance in the grand scheme of things. And when a writer like Herman Melville dips his quill in seawater it is to stir up a longing for a life on the ocean wave he had lived for real. Run your finger along his words and taste it. The salt will sting your lips.

The watery words in this collection have been distilled from sources as varied as the sea itself, including classic adventure yarns, nursery rhymes and ancient texts. The old scripts speak to us as powerfully as the modern since the sea, unlike the landscape, has changed so little over the centuries. The Aegean we gaze upon today is more or less the same Aegean Homer gazed upon nearly three thousand years ago when he coined the phrase 'wine-dark sea.' Come to that, it's more or less the same Aegean prehistoric man gazed upon. The sea connects us to our past like nothing else on earth.

You might think that choosing watery images to complement the words would be a breeze; after all, it's virtually impossible to take a poor photograph of the sea. Like Marilyn Monroe, the sea is endlessly photogenic, isn't it? It is, and therein lies the problem. The sea has become rather a visual cliché. Crashing waves, picturesque coastlines, bobbing fishing boats, yeah, yeah, been there, seen that, in every tourist brochure and on every seaside postcard this side of Cape Cod.

To capture the true spirit of the ocean takes an artist's eye. Master lensmen like Ernst Haas, Warren Bolster and Henry Lytton Cobbold not only possess a technical mastery of their medium but that artist's eye which sees past surface beauty to what lies beneath. Black and white is the perfect way to see the sea, as it takes you straight to the heart of the subject by focusing on pattern, texture, light and shade. And, like the sea, black and white is timeless.

With such capable 'crew,' the voyage ahead is sure to be exhilarating and enlightening. Charting a course from Cornwall to the Caribbean, you'll sample the varied delights of ocean life, splashing and sailing, surfing and swimming, and simply staring out upon shimmering seas fringed with palms like the eyelashes of a beautiful woman. Along the way, you'll enjoy the lively company of ambassadors of the deep such as dolphins, whales, mermaids and tigers. Tigers? Wait and see… surprises are part of the package. More than just a cruise down memory lane, this is a voyage of discovery – and self-discovery. "For whatever we lose (like a you or a me) it's always ourselves we find in the sea," wrote E.E. Cummings. Answer the call of the sea and who knows what treasures you will find. Anchors aweigh!

BEHOLD THE SEA!

And behold the sea,
the opaline, plentiful and strong,
yet beautiful as the rose in June
or the trickling rainbow,
full of food,
nourisher of men,
purger of the world,
creating a sweet climate,
and in its unchangeable ebb and flow
and in its beauty at a few furlongs,
giving a hint of that which changeth not
and is perfect.

Ralph Waldo Emerson

THE SEA

The sea! the sea! the open sea!
The blue, the fresh, the ever free!
Without a mark, without a bound,
It runneth the earth's wide regions round!
It plays with the clouds; it mocks the skies;
Or like a cradled creature lies.

I'm on the sea! I'm on the sea!
I am where I would ever be;
With the blue above, and the blue below,
And silence wheresoe'er I go;
If a storm should come and awake the deep,
What matter? I shall ride and sleep.

Barry Cornwall

COME WHITE HORSES

Now my brothers call from the bay
Now the great winds shorewards blow
Now the salt tides seawards flow
Now the wild white horses play,
Champ and chafe and toss in the spray.

Matthew Arnold

Give me this glorious ocean life, this salt-sea life,
this briny, foamy life, when the sea neighs and snorts,
and you breathe the very breath that the great whales respire!
Let me roll around the globe, let me rock upon the sea;
let me race and pant out my life, with an eternal breeze astern,
and an endless sea before!

Herman Melville

SALTY SEA FACTS

The oceans cover 71 per cent of the total area of the earth, and contain enough water to cover the entire planet to a depth of 2.7 km (1¾ miles) if the surface were completely flat.

Joshua Slocum, the first person to sail solo around the world, was a non-swimmer.

The Inuit-Eskimo people may have dozens of names for snow, but the Torres Strait Islanders native to the northern coasts of Australia, have more than 80 words to describe different tides.

Beethoven composed all his music without ever having looked upon the sea.

A message in a bottle thrown into the sea from the SS Arawatta in Queensland, Australia, was washed ashore on nearby Moreton Island, 73 years later. (It read, "No milk today, please.")

There are estimated to be 14,700 000 000 000 000 tons of salt in the oceans. If all the ocean water evaporated and the salt was spread evenly over the whole earth, the pile of salt would be as high as a 15-storey building.

Harbours are not necessarily safe havens. More people fall overboard while in harbour than at sea.

Only drummer, Dennis Wilson, of the Beach Boys, actually surfed.

The seabed is not flat. It has mountain ranges, and valleys called canyons and trenches.

If the oceans were shared equally among everyone on the planet, we would all receive 100 billion gallons of water each.

BEACHCOMBING

Memory is a child walking along a seashore.
You never know what small pebble it will pick
up and store away with its treasured things.

Pierce Harris

Every time we walk along a beach some ancient
urge disturbs us so that we find ourselves shedding
shoes and garments or scavenging among seaweed
and whitened timbers like the homesick refugees of
a long war.

Loren Eiseley

on the low-tide beach,
everything we pick up
moves

Chiyo-Ni

I DO LIKE TO BE BESIDE THE SEASIDE

Oh! I do like to be beside the seaside
I do like to be beside the sea
I do like to stroll upon the Prom, Prom, Prom,
Where the brass bands play
Tiddely om pom pom!
So just let me be beside the seaside
I'll be beside myself with glee
And there's lots of girls beside,
I should like to be beside,
Beside the seaside!
Beside the sea!

John A. Glover-Kind

I SCREAM, YOU SCREAM…

Ice cream is as much a part of the seaside-experience as buckets and spades and soggy swimsuits. The story goes that this cooling treat was invented in A.D 54 by the Roman Emperor, Nero. He sent fleet-footed slaves up into the mountains to collect snow which was then delivered to the palace chefs who flavoured it with wine, honey or fruit. These days, Americans have the greatest love affair with ice cream, spending 20 billion dollars a year (not each!). And the best-selling flavour is… vanilla.

I doubt whether the world holds for anyone a more soul-stirring surprise than the first adventure with ice cream.

Heywood Broun

Age does not diminish the extreme disappointment of having a scoop of ice cream fall from the cone.

Jim Freiburg

Life is like an ice-cream cone. You have to lick it one day at a time.

Charlie Brown

NEWS FLASH

A young girl who was blown out to sea
on a set of inflatable teeth was rescued
by a man on an inflatable lobster.
A coastguard spokesman commented,
"This sort of thing is all too common."

The Times

SEASIDE TONGUE TWISTERS

She sells sea-shells on the sea shore,
The shells she sells are sea-shells I'm sure,
So if she sells sea-shells on the sea shore,
I'm sure that the shells are sea-shore shells.

Swan swam over the sea,
Swim, swan, swim!
Swan swam back again,
Well swum swan!

Selfish shellfish. Selfish shellfish. Selfish shellfish.

A sailor went to sea, sea, sea,
To see what he could see, see, see.
But all that he could see, see, see
Was the bottom of the deep blue sea, sea, sea.

Never a ship sails out a bay, but carries my heart as a stowaway.

Roselle Mercier Montgomery

TIGER, TIGER...

These are the times of dreamy quietude, when
beholding the tranquil beauty and brilliancy of the
ocean's skin, one forgets the tiger heart that pants
beneath it, and would not willingly remember, that
this velvet paw but conceals a remorseless fang.

Herman Melville

The sea is feline. It licks your feet – its huge flanks
purr very pleasantly for you; but it will crack your
bones and eat you, for all that, and wipe your
crimson foam from its jaw as if nothing had happened.

Oliver Wendell Holmes

My lips will feast on the foam of thy lips,
I shall rise with thy rising, with thee subside.

Algernon Charles Swinburne

SEA OF SENSUALITY

Cushion me soft
Rock me in billowy drowse
Dash me with amorous wet

Walt Whitman

I will be the waves
you will be a strange shore.
I shall roll on and on and on
and break upon your lap with laughter.

Rabindranath Tagore

DOVER BEACH

The sea is calm tonight.
The tide is full, the moon lies fair
Upon the straits; – on the French coast the light
Gleams and is gone; the cliffs of England stand
Glimmering and vast, out in the tranquil bay.
Come to the window, sweet is the night-air!
Only, from the long line of spray
Where the sea meets the moon-blanch'd land,
Listen! you hear the grating roar
Of pebbles which the waves draw back, and fling,
At their return, up the high strand,
Begin, and cease, and then again begin,
With tremulous cadence slow, and bring
The eternal note of sadness in.

Matthew Arnold

NAUTICAL NONSENSE AND WATERY WIT

I have a large seashell collection, which I keep scattered on beaches all over the world.
Steven Wright

He had bought a large map representing the sea
without the least vestige of land:
And the crew were much pleased when they found it to be
A map they could all understand.
Edward Lear

I can never remember if Moby Dick is the man or the whale.
James Thurber

I once built a ship in a bottle. They had to break the bottle to let me out.
Steven Wright

When Scottish people take their clothes off at the seaside, they're blue, and it takes a whole week of sunbathing to become white.
Billy Connolly

Three wise men of Gotham
Went to sea in a bowl;
If the bowl had been stronger,
My story would have been longer.
Mother Goose

A sure cure for seasickness is to sit under a tree.
Spike Milligan

When I go to the beach wearing a bikini, even the tide won't come in.
Phyllis Diller

How on earth did Gandhi manage to walk so far in flip-flops?
When I'm at the seaside, I can't last ten minutes in mine.
Mrs Merton

What are the vital statistics of a mermaid? 36: 24: and 95 pence a pound.
Anon

MESSING ABOUT IN BOATS

There is *nothing* – absolutely nothing – half so much
worth doing as simply messing about in boats.
Kenneth Grahame

Land was created to provide a place for boats to visit.
Brooks Atkinson

My idea of having fun in a boat is to get as far away
from telephones as possible.
Roderick Stephens

I don't own a boat, but I have a lot of friends with boats, which
anyone can tell you is a lot better.
Robert Stone

DANCES WITH WAVES

Come unto these yellow sands,
And then take hands:
Court'sied when you have, and kiss'd, –
The wild waves whist, –
Foot it featly here and there;
And, sweet sprites, the burthen bear.

William Shakespeare

I was born by the sea, and I have noticed that all of
the great events of my life have taken place by the sea.
My first idea of movement, of the dance, certainly came
from the rhythm of the waves. As a child I danced on
the sea beach. The movement of the waves rocked with
my soul. Could I dance as they, their eternal message
of rhythm and harmony?

Isadora Duncan

SEA KISSES

She lifted her face suddenly to him,
and he touched it with his lips.
So cold, so fresh, so sea-clear her face was,
it was like kissing a flower that grows near the surf.

D. H. Lawrence

He kissed her and promised.
Such beautiful lips!
Man's usual fate –
He was lost upon the coral reefs.

Douglas Jerrold

SKIMMING STONES

The Americans call it 'dabbing,' the French call it 'ricochet,' and the British – for reasons unknown – call it 'ducks and drakes.' Whatever you call it, the ancient game of skimming stones across water is still popular on beaches across the world. Nine or ten bounces may make you a hero among your friends but to beat the current Guinness World Stone Skipping Record you need to achieve a cool 41 skips.

The secret of stone-skimming success is wrapped up in a mathematical formula that is classified information since the same principle is used to bounce intercontinental ballistic missiles in space. It was a game of ducks and drakes with his grandchildren that gave British engineer, Dr. Barnes Wallis, the idea for the 'bouncing bomb' used during World War II.

If you're keen to improve your technique, here are a few tips that won't contravene the Official Secrets Act: Pick a flat stone of equal thickness, no bigger than the palm of your hand. Hold the stone between your thumb and middle finger and position yourself at an angle to the water, crouching low. With a sharp flick of the wrist, throw out and down, as parallel to the water as possible. The faster the spinning stone travels the more times it will bounce.

SEA VIEW

No shoes, no shirt...no problem
Sign on seafront-café, Barbados

There is, perhaps, no better way to hold communion with the sea than sitting in the sun on the veranda of a fisherman's café.
Joseph W. Beach

Lovely it is, when the winds are stirring up the waves on the sea, to gaze out from the land on the great efforts of someone else.
Lucretius

THE SEA IS LIKE…

The sea was sparkling like joy itself.
Christopher Isherwood

There the sea I found
Calm as a cradled child in dreamless slumber bound.
Percy Bysshe Shelley

The sea, like a crinkled chart, spread to the horizon.
Daphne du Maurier

Long blue rollers came in, each a neat and level line like an ironed crease.
George Garrett

The water of Sydney Harbour is like silk, like pewter, like blood, like a
leopard's skin, and occasionally merely like water.
Kenneth Slessor

The sea, like a great sultan, supports thousands of ships, his lawful wives.
Felix Reisenberg

I liked to sail alone. The sea was like a girl to me – I did not want anyone
else along.
E. B. White

The sea was angry that day, my friends. Like an old man trying to send
back soup in a deli.
Seinfeld

Here we are becalmed, the sea looking like a plate of silver that has been
cleaned by a remarkably good under-butler. He has not left a spot on it.
Emily Eden

The sea made small lapping sounds, as if a kindly monster was taking
discreet sips of water from a large goblet.
Alain de Botton

HEAVENLY SEA

I ran like a boy, tore off my clothes, and hurled myself in the water. And I was in Heaven! The whole sea was literally golden as well as green – it was liquid and living sunlight in which one lived and moved and had one's being. And to feel that in deep water is to feel—as long as one is swimming out, if only a minute or two—as if one was in another world of life, and one far more glorious than even Dante ever dreamed of in his paradise.

Charles Algernon Swinburne

How the water sports and sings!
(surely it is alive!)

Walt Whitman

GONE FISHIN'

If people concentrated on the really important things in life,
there'd be a shortage of fishing poles.
Doug Larson

I love fishing. It's transcendental meditation with a punchline.
Billy Connolly

Many men go fishing their entire lives without knowing it is
not fish they are after.
Henry David Thoreau

I fish because mercifully there are no telephones on fishing waters; because
bourbon out of an old tin cup always tastes better out there; because maybe
one day I will catch a mermaid…
Robert Traver

There's a fine line between fishing and just standing on the shore looking
like an idiot.
Steven Wright

THE LITTLE MERMAID

Far out in the wide sea, where the water is blue as the prettiest cornflower, and clear as the purest crystal, it is very, very deep; so deep, indeed, that many church steeples, piled one upon another, would not reach from the lowest depth to the surface of the water above. Here dwells the Mer-King and his subjects…

The Mer-King had six beautiful children; but the youngest was the loveliest of all; her skin was as soft and delicate as a rose-leaf, and her eyes as blue as the deepest sea; but, like all other mermaids, she had no feet, and her body ended in a fish's tail. All day long the children played in the great halls of the Sea Palace, where beautiful flowers grew out of the walls and fish swam through great amber windows…

Hans Christian Anderson

WHALES WEEP NOT!

They say the sea is cold, but the sea contains
the hottest blood of all, and the wildest, the most urgent.

All the whales in the wider deeps, hot are they, as they urge
on and on, and dive beneath the icebergs.
The right whales, the sperm-whales, the hammer-heads, the killers
there they blow, there they blow, hot wild white breath out of
the sea!

And they rock, and they rock, through the sensual ageless ages
on the depths of the seven seas,
and through the salt they reel with drunk delight
and in the tropics tremble they with love
and roll with massive, strong desire, like gods…

D. H. Lawrence

SEA OF WORDS

Britain was a maritime empire, so many seafaring expressions have washed ashore into the English language. The maritime origins of phrases like 'plain sailing,' 'learn the ropes,' and 'hit the deck' are instantly clear, but here's a selection of everyday expressions whose nautical roots are less obvious…

SHAKE A LEG
This wake-up call dates back to the age of sailing ships when women often spent the night on board ship. In the morning, at reveille, a woman would display a smooth, shapely leg from the hammock thus entitling her to a lie-in.

SQUARE MEAL
The ship's crew ate their meals off square, wooden platters because they were easier to stow than round ones.

MONEY FOR OLD ROPE
In the days of sail, sailors were permitted to unravel used and unwanted rope and sell it on shore for use as caulking.

NO ROOM TO SWING A CAT

When an insubordinate crew member had to undergo a lashing, all hands were summoned on deck to bear witness to the punishment. This made for a crowded deck – so crowded that there was often no room to swing the cat o' nine tails without hitting spectators.

SLUSH FUND

Slush was the name for the waste fat from the galley of a ship. A slush fund was the money accumulated by the ship's cook from the collection and sale of slush.

AS THE CROW FLIES

Crows hate large open spaces of water and instinctively head straight towards the nearest land. Ships routinely carried a cage of crows, which could be released in foggy waters to point the way to land. (This is why the lookout platform on the ship's mast came to be known as the crow's nest.)

CRUISING

A girl never really looks as well as she does on board a steamship or a yacht.
Anita Loos

If you have to ask how much it costs, you can't afford one.
J. P. Morgan

With all the unrest in the world, I don't think anybody should have a yacht
that sleeps more than twelve.
Tony Curtis, Some Like It Hot

I entertained on a cruising trip that was so much fun that I had to sink my
yacht to make my guests go home.
F. Scott Fitzgerald

THE SECRET

In the profoundest ocean
There is a rainbow shell,
It is always there, shining most stilly
Under the greatest storm waves
That the old Greek called "ripples of laughter."
As you listen, the rainbow shell
Sings—in the profoundest ocean.
It is always there, singing most silently!

Katherine Mansfield

ETERNAL SEA

There is something in being near the sea,
like the confines of eternity. It is a new
element, a pure abstraction. The mind
loves to hover on that which is endless,
and forever the same.

I wonder at the sea, that vast Leviathan,
rolled round the earth, smiling in its sleep,
waked into fury, fathomless, boundless,
a huge world of water-drops – Whence is it,
whither goes it, is it of eternity or of nothing?

William Hazlitt

THE SEA GYPSY

I am fevered with the sunset,
I am fretful with the bay,
For the wander-thirst is on me
And my soul in Cathay.

There's a schooner in the offing,
With the topsails shot with fire,
And my heart has gone aboard her
For the Islands of Desire.

I must forth again to-morrow!
With the sunset I must be
Hull down on the trail of rapture
In the wonder of the sea.

Richard Hovey

SAILING

Why do I sail? Because the water is endless: once you set out you are free of where you were and linked to everywhere else. Because the gurgle of water under the forefoot is both lullaby and promise of things to come. Because on the ocean you know there won't be anyone to meet, no egos to contend with but your own. And because of the connection and connectedness. From millions of miles away, the stars tell you where you are, while nearby the porpoises and whales tell you there is company for your soul. The permanent impermanence of the ocean itself banishes 'I' and reaffirms 'I am.'

Entry from the log of a sailor on an Atlantic crossing

The hardest part of sailing round the world? Stepping onto dry land.

Ellen MacArthur

They came unto a land in which it seemed always afternoon.

Alfred Lord Tennyson

SEA DREAMS

Sit in reverie
and
watch
the changing colour
of the waves
that break
upon
the idle seashore
of the mind

H. W. Longfellow

THE FLOATING WORLD

I am the pool of blue
That worships the vivid sky;
My hopes were heaven-high,
They are all fulfilled in you.

Sara Teasdale

The voice of the sea speaks to the soul.
The touch of the sea is sensuous,
enfolding the body in its soft close embrace.

Kate Chopin

SEA WISDOM

You will never discover new oceans unless you have the courage to lose sight of the shore.
English Proverb

The seaweed is always greener in somebody else's lake.
Sebastian, Disney's The Little Mermaid

If your ship doesn't come in, swim out to it!
Jonathan Winters

How inappropriate to call this planet Earth when it is clearly Ocean.
Arthur C. Clarke

The cure for anything is saltwater – sweat, tears, or the sea.
Isak Dinesen

SWIMMING WITH DOLPHINS

Of the two smartest creatures on the earth, man and the dolphin, each thought they were smarter than the other. Man thought he was smarter because he built many things and did much work, while the dolphins just played all day. The dolphins thought they were smarter for the same reason.
Gershon Legman

It is of interest to note that while some dolphins are reported to have learned English—up to fifty words used in correct context—no human being has been reported to have learned dolphinese.
Carl Sagan

I plan to be reincarnated as a dolphin.
Margo Oberg, World Surfing Champion

AND I HAVE LOVED THEE, OCEAN!

And I have loved thee, Ocean! and my joy
Of youthful sports was on thy breast to be
Borne, like thy bubbles, onward; from a boy
I wantoned with thy breakers,—they to me
Were a delight; and if the freshening sea
Made them a terror, 'twas a pleasing fear,
For I was as it were a child of thee,
And trusted to thy billows far and near,
And laid my hand upon thy mane
– as I do here.

Lord Byron

A TOAST

Here's to tall ships
Here's to small ships
Here's to all the ships on the sea
But the best ships are friendships –
Here's to you and me.

Anon

MY BONNIE LIES OVER THE OCEAN

My Bonnie lies over the ocean
My Bonnie lies over the sea,
My Bonnie lies over the ocean,
Oh bring back my Bonnie to me.

Bring back, bring back,
Oh bring back my Bonnie to me, to me,
Bring back, bring back,
Oh bring back my Bonnie to me.

The winds have blown over the ocean,
The winds have blown over the sea;
The winds have blown over the ocean,
and brought back my Bonnie to me.

Traditional

Credits

About the author

Rosemarie Jarski is a writer and lifelong sea-lover. She tries to compensate for not living by the sea by adding salt to her bath-water and sleeping on a waterbed. Last year she swam the Hellespont.

First published in 2005 by
New Holland Publishers (UK) Ltd
London • Cape Town • Sydney • Auckland
www.newhollandpublishers.com

Garfield House, 86–88 Edgware Road
London W2 2EA United Kingdom

80 McKenzie Street
Cape Town 8001 South Africa

14 Aquatic Drive
Frenchs Forest, NSW 2086 Australia

218 Lake Road
Northcote, Auckland New Zealand

1 3 5 7 9 10 8 6 4 2

ISBN 1 84330 980 7

Senior Editor: Clare Hubbard
Editorial Direction: Rosemary Wilkinson
Design: Paul Wright
Production: Ben Byram-Wigfield

Reproduction by Modern Age Repro House Ltd, Hong Kong
Printed and bound by Craft Print International Pte Ltd, Singapore

When he left the beach the sea was still going on.

Derek Walcott